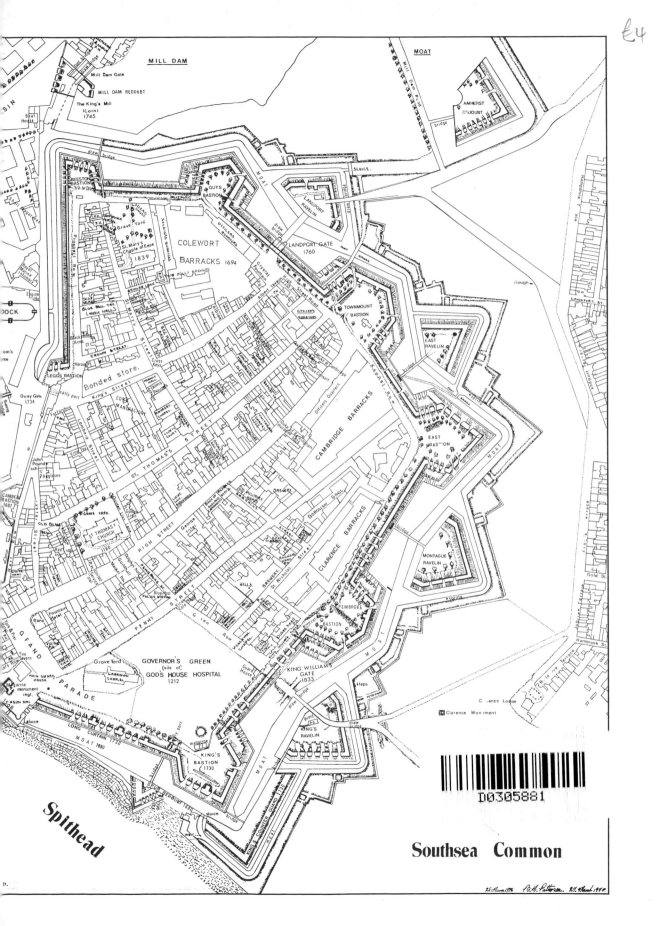

£4

MILL DAM

MOAT

Spithead

Southsea Common

# Bygone
# PORTSMOUTH

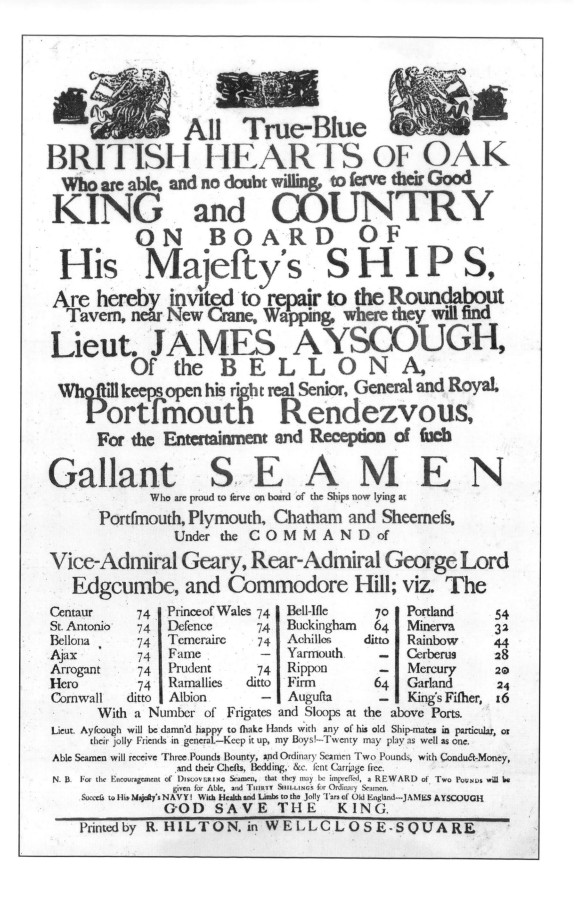

# Bygone
# PORTSMOUTH

## Peter Rogers and David Francis

## Phillimore

1994

Published by
PHILLIMORE & CO. LTD.
Shopwyke Manor Barn, Chichester, Sussex

© Peter Rogers and David Francis, 1994

ISBN 0 85033 920 0

Printed and bound in Great Britain by
BIDDLES LTD.
Guildford, Surrey

# List of Illustrations

*Frontispiece:* Royal Navy recruiting poster

# PORTSMOUTH
## A Reader's Guide

A full history of Portsmouth is beyond the scope of this book. Many books and papers have appeared which partially do the job. Some of these are works of genuine scholarship, others journalistic hackwork of little reliability. We have attempted here no more than the briefest of brief summaries, but have provided references where the interested reader can find more information. Many of the items cited are out of print, but those no longer available in good bookshops should be readily obtainable through the public library service.

The definitive history of Portsmouth has yet to be written, and none of the attempts to do so is, at the time of writing, in print. For some account of the pre-1900 histories of Portsmouth see:

Webb, John, 'Young antiquaries: Lake Allen and Frederic Madden', in Webb, John, Yates, Nigel and Peacock, Sarah (eds.), *Hampshire Studies*, Portsmouth: Portsmouth City Records Office, 1981, especially pp. 202-3 and 211-12, and also Mr. Webb's *Sir Frederic Madden and Portsmouth*, Portsmouth Papers No 47, Portsmouth: Portsmouth City Council, 1987.

Among histories written since the turn of the century, mention may be made of the following:

Gates, William G., *Illustrated History of Portsmouth*, Portsmouth: Charpentier and Co.; Evening News and Hampshire Telegraph Company, 1900. A worthy effort at a comprehensive history, but the author was primarily a newspaper man, and secondarily a historian; his eye for a good story took precedent over scrupulous scholarship, and the book contains many inaccuracies. (See Webb, J., 'Portsmouth and its past' in Webb, J. *et al.*, *The Spirit of Portsmouth: A History*, Chichester: Phillimore and Co. Ltd., 1989, pp. 160-1.)

Sparks, Henry J., *The Story of Portsmouth*, Portsmouth: Charpentier and Co., 1921. An illustrated history aimed at school children by a lecturer in history at Portsmouth Municipal College.

Lipscomb, F.W., *Heritage of Sea Power: the Story of Portsmouth*, London: Hutchinson, 1967. A popular, illustrated history, but concentrating on naval and military affairs.

Patterson, A. Temple, *Portsmouth: a history*, Bradford-on-Avon: Moonraker Press, 1976. Blurb claims it as a 'modern and comprehensive history', but severely criticised in *Portsmouth Archives Review*, 2, 1977 for drawing on unreliable sources.

*Portsmouth through the Centuries*, Portsmouth: Portsmouth City Records Office, 1979. A very sound summary history of Portsmouth, regrettably allowed to go out of print.

Two recent volumes that are collections of essays on various aspects of Portsmouth's history by authors of academic standing are:

Webb, J. *et al., The Spirit of Portsmouth: A History*, Chichester: Phillimore & Co. Ltd., 1989.

Stapleton, Barry and Thomas, James H. (eds.), *The Portsmouth Region*, Gloucester: Alan Sutton, 1989.

Two publications which present events in Portsmouth's history in a chronological arrangement are:

Gates, William G., *The Portsmouth that has Passed with Glimpses of God's Port: A Panorama of a Thousand Years*, Portsmouth: Portsmouth and Sunderland Newspapers, Ltd., ?1946. Illustrations and notes on interesting events from 491 B.C. to 1941. This was republished by Milestone Press of Horndean in 1987, edited by Nigel Peake.

Bishop, Graham, *Portsmouth Pageant*, Portsmouth: Portsmouth City Council, 1983. Notes on the principal events from A.D. 44.

Worth referring to for recent history is the Portsmouth Corporation Records Series. In a number of volumes covering the years 1835 to date, by various editors, they provide a chronological, and latterly thematic account of the major events in Portsmouth's history.

Domesday Book (1086) mentions manors at Bocheland (Buckland), Copenore (Copnor) and Frodintone (Fratton) on Portsea Island, and a church (St Mary's) was built to serve them probably in 1164. But Portsmouth really grew up in the area we now know as Old Portsmouth, where the Norman merchant John de Gisors, presumably availing himself of the Camber as a harbour, granted land for St Thomas's church around 1180.

The best account of the early history of Portsmouth is:

Quail, Sarah, *The Origins of Portsmouth and the First Charter*, Portsmouth: Portsmouth City Council, 1994.

Reference may also usefully be made to Hoad, Margaret, 'The Origins of Portsmouth' in Webb, John, Yates, Nigel, and Peacock, Sarah (eds.), *Hampshire Studies*, Portsmouth: Portsmouth City Records Office, 1981, pp. 1-30.

King Alfred is said to have used Portsmouth harbour as a base in the ninth century, and its advantages became apparent to many other kings subsequently, including King Harold, William the Conqueror, Henry I and II, Richard I, John, Henry III, Edward I, Edward II, Henry V and Henry VIII, who all used it as an embarkation or disembarkation point at some time during their reigns.

There are numerous books pertaining to the history of the navy and individual vessels, and the Portsmouth District Central Library holds a major collection of such material. Works of specifically local significance include:

Sparks, Henry J., *A Naval History of Portsmouth*, Portsmouth: Charpentier and Co., 1912. This claims to have used a wide range of primary sources.

Gates, William G., *History of Portsmouth: A Naval Chronology*, Portsmouth: Evening News and Hampshire Telegraph Co., 1931. A copious work, but statements of fact would repay independent verification.

Warner, Oliver, *Portsmouth and the Royal Navy*, Portsmouth: Gale and Polden Limited, 1965. A glossy publication, issued in the year the Royal Navy was given the freedom of Portsmouth.

Lewis, Michael, *Spithead: an Informal History*, London: George Allen and Unwin Ltd., 1972. An illustrated account written by an eminent naval historian.

Webb, John, *The City of Portsmouth and the Royal Navy*, London: Pitkin Pictorials Ltd., 1984. A lavishly illustrated pamphlet by a scholarly historian.

The interested reader is also recommended to keep up with the publications of the Dockyard Historical Society.

As Portsmouth became important as a naval base, it attracted raids from the French. There were several in the 14th century and, as a result, increasingly substantial fortifications were erected round the town and were eventually dominated by the Round and Square Towers (1417 and 1494 respectively). The fortifications reached their maximum extent at the end of the 17th century.

Many items have been published about the fortifications. Among recent contributions the following can be suggested:

Corney, Arthur, *Fortifications in Old Portsmouth: a Guide*, Portsmouth: Portsmouth City Museums, 1965.

Patterson, A. Temple, *'Palmerston's Folly': the Portsdown and Spithead Forts*, Portsmouth Papers No 3; Portsmouth: Portsmouth City Council, 1968. As much concerned with political considerations as with fabric.

Hogg, Ian V., *Coast defences of England and Wales 1856-1956*, Newton Abbot: David and Charles, 1974, pp. 121-67.

Powell, Michael, *Spithead: the Navy's Anvil*, Redan and Vedette, 1977. A detailed history of the fortifications with a layman's guide as to how they functioned.

Quail, Sarah, 'Stone towers: the fortifications of Portsmouth' in Webb, J. *et al., The Spirit of Portsmouth: A History*, Chichester: Phillimore, 1989, pp. 53-67.

The interested reader is also recommended to keep up with a series called The Solent Papers, each devoted to the study of a particular fort or forts.

It should be recalled at this point that we are still discussing the area known today as Old Portsmouth; the only other habitation on Portsea Island was in a few scattered farms and tiny villages. By the start of the 18th century, the area within the walls of (old) Portsmouth was becoming very congested, and permission was at length given for building to take place on Portsea Common (the area around what is now Queen Street), and a new town quickly developed there (see, for example, Harwood, Joy, *A Portrait of Portsea 1840-1940*, Southampton: Ensign Publications, 1990). Portsea was provided with extensive fortifications of its own as late as the 1770s, making it almost certainly the last place in the world to be equipped with city walls, basically a medieval military concept!

Southsea began life in the early 19th century, more as a haven for retired and half-pay officers than as a sea-side resort. The earliest parts of Southsea are in fact the terraces (Hampshire, King's, Jubilee and Bellevue), built just outside the confines of the fortifications, to provide more pleasant dwellings with more space than was by then possible within them. The growth of Southsea was stimulated by the activities of Thomas Ellis Owen, architect/property developer/local politician who speculatively built many of the houses in the Palmerston Road area, and provided St Jude's church for the wealthy residents.

For accounts of the history of Southsea, see, for example:

Riley, R.C., *The Growth of Southsea as a Naval Satellite and Victorian Resort*, Portsmouth Papers No 16; Portsmouth: Portsmouth City Council, 1972

Curtis, William and Villar, Diana, *Southsea: its Story*, Alresford: Bay Tree Publishing Company, 1978. Pleasantly written popular history giving way to personal reminiscences.

For Owen's activities, see Riley, R.C., *The Houses and Inhabitants of Thomas Ellis Owen's Southsea*, Portsmouth Papers No 32; Portsmouth: Portsmouth City Council, 1980.

The railway, initially from the Brighton direction, reached Portsmouth in 1847 and as the population increased rapidly with the importance of the dockyard, building soon stretched eastwards and northwards across the island, so that, by the turn of the 20th century, the areas to the south of the railway, and to the west of it as far as North End, were all built up. Most of the rest of the available space was filled between the wars.

The first significant change in the appearance of Portsmouth, other than the inevitable growth and improvement of some the buildings over the years, was the demolition of the fortifications in the 1870s. Some slum clearance, especially in the Portsea area, took place in the 1930s. (For some account of that, see Allaway, A.E., 'The Housing and Slum Clearance Problem in Portsmouth', *Journal of the Royal Sanitary Institute*, 55(1), July 1934, pp. 38-45.)

The biggest changes of all were wrought by Hitler's bombs, and a number of books about Portsmouth in the Second World War have appeared, for example:

*Smitten City: The Story of Portsmouth in the Air Raids 1940-1944*, Portsmouth: the Evening News, ?1945. An album of views of air raid damage to Portsmouth, with notes, compiled from the files of the local paper. The book was re-issued in 1981, with a small number of changes in the illustrations.

*Portsmouth at War*, Portsmouth: W.E.A. Local History Group; 3 vols, 1983, *c*.1987 and 1990. Miscellaneous personal reminiscences.

Jenkins, Paul, *Battle over Portsmouth: a City at War in 1940*, Midhurst: Middleton Press, 1986. A blow by blow account of the events of 1940, with many illustrations.

Peake, Nigel, *City at War: a Pictorial Memento of Portsmouth, Gosport, Fareham, Havant and Chichester during World War II*, Horndean: Milestone Publications, 1986. Mainly illustrations with informative linking chapters.

Post-war redevelopment, road construction and pedestrianisation have further contributed to changes in the townscape. For example, who would think, just looking at the current scene, that King's Road before the war was a fashionable shopping area, or that less than a generation ago there were bus stops more or less at the foot of the Guildhall steps?

Many aspects of Portsmouth's history have been written up at some time. Portsmouth City Council's Portsmouth Papers (cited several times here) reliably cover a wide range of historical topics, and local libraries and record offices are always most helpful in suggesting other appropriate material. Our account concludes with a brief look at some items which evoke various aspects of the Portsmouth scene in days gone by.

Published works about buildings naturally concentrate on those that their authors regarded as important or significant. The following three items all deal with buildings extant at their time of writing, although some changes have occurred since they were published.

Pevsner, Nikolaus, and Lloyd, David, *Hampshire and the Isle of Wight*, Harmondsworth: Penguin Books Ltd., 1967. One of Penguin's Buildings of England series, Portsmouth is dealt with on pp. 389-470.

Balfour, Alan, *Portsmouth*, London: Studio Vista, 1970. One of Studio Vista's City Buildings series; illustrations and notes (sometimes in incomprehensible architectural jargon) on 170 buildings in the Portsmouth area.

Lloyd, David, *Buildings of Portsmouth and its Environs: a Survey of the Dockyard, Defences, Homes, Churches, Commercial, Civic and Public Buildings*, Portsmouth: Portsmouth City Council, 1974. Contains much of interest.

Dealing with particular types of large, easily noticed buildings that have some literature devoted to them, in alphabetical order we come first to **churches**. Most churches have their individual guide-books and/or histories; some, for example the Anglican Cathedral and St Mary's, Portsea, have had several items written about them. Works that attempt an account of a number of churches are:

Hubbuck, Rodney, *Portsea Island Churches*, Portsmouth Papers No 8; Portsmouth: Portsmouth City Council, 1969. Concentrates on architecture, and few non-Anglican churches are dealt with. There was a slightly revised edition in 1976.

Offord, John, *Churches, Chapels and Places of Worship on Portsea Island*, Southsea: John Harman, 1989. Lively and informative; while strongest on Anglican and Catholic churches, the establishments of some non-Christian groups are also considered.

Quail, Sarah, 'The way people worshipped', in Webb, J. *et al.*, *The Spirit of Portsmouth: A History*, Chichester: Phillimore, 1989, pp. 100-20. A summary of Christian and Jewish worship.

It is perhaps surprising that the **cinemas** of Portsmouth have had relatively little attention. The only attempt at a comprehensive account to have come to light is:

Barker, J., Brown, R., and Greer, W., *The Cinemas of Portsmouth*, Horndean: Milestone Publications, 2nd revised edn. 1982. Contains a lot of interesting information and illustrations, perhaps marred by an ultra-popular style of presentation.

As with the cinemas, so with the **hospitals**; the one overall survey is:

Gange, Molly, *The Hospitals of Portsmouth Past and Present*, Southampton: Ensign Publications, 1988. A lot of detail in a small space, but could have done with more rigorous editing.

An account of the **housing** in Portsmouth is probably too large an undertaking for a single work. A number of articles have appeared in the town planning or architectural press about particular developments, but one to consider historical aspects of working class housing (so typical of Portsmouth and what makes the townscape so different from almost all other places on the south coast) is:

Freeman, M.D., 'Working-class Housing in Portsmouth', *Industrial Archaeology*, 10(2), May 1973, pp. 152-60. An illustrated account of the different styles of artisan dwellings built in the 19th century.

The history of **industrial buildings** is best summed up in:

Riley, R.C., *The Industrial Archaeology of the Portsmouth Region*, Portsmouth Papers No 48; Portsmouth: Portsmouth City Council, 1987. A copiously documented work.

The most ubiquitous type of non-residential building in Portsmouth, probably even now and certainly in the pre-war years, was the public house. There were few if any places in the country where the provision per head of population was greater! Two contrasting items evoke the **pubs** of Portsmouth in the past:

Riley, R.C. and, Eley, Philip, *Public Houses and Beerhouses in Nineteenth Century Portsmouth*, Portsmouth Papers No 38; Portsmouth: Portsmouth City Council, 1983. A scholarly account.

Brown, Ron, *The Pubs of Portsmouth*, Horndean: Milestone Publications, 1985. A list of streets with notes on the pubs they contained, with some interesting old photographs.

Last in our consideration of significant buildings of Portsmouth comes **theatres**. Again, two items offer themselves to the interested reader:

Sargeant, Harry, *A History of Portsmouth Theatres*, Portsmouth Papers No 13; Portsmouth: Portsmouth City Council, 1971.

Offord, John, *The Theatres of Portsmouth*, Horndean: Milestone Publications, 1983. Includes mention of some that were mooted but never came to fruition.

There are of course other large buildings—garages, shops, educational establishments, for instance—which, while certain individual examples have had their chroniclers, have yet to be given comprehensive treatment. But the various aspects of **public transport** may be considered as part of the townscape.

**Buses** and **trams** have been given a great deal of attention by enthusiasts, and Portsmouth District Central Library has a number of fleet lists and similar publications. The more substantial contributions to the history of road transport in Portsmouth include:

Harrison, S.E., *The Tramways of Portsmouth*, London: the Light Railway Transport League, 2nd edn. 1963. A detailed well-illustrated monograph.

Janes, D.A.P., and Funnell, R.G., *The Trolleybuses of Portsmouth: a Comprehensive History of the Portsmouth Trolley Bus System, with complete fleet details, and a record of sold vehicles*, Reading: the Reading Transport Society, 1969. Chronological account with a number of illustrations.

John, Malcolm, *Portsmouth Buses*, Chatham: Rochester Press, 1983. Some 65 captioned photographs, mainly 1930s to date.

Course, Edwin, *Portsmouth Corporation Tramways 1896-1936*, Portsmouth Papers No 45; Portsmouth: Portsmouth City Council, 1986.

Watts, Eric, *Fares Please: the History of Passenger Transport in Portsmouth*, Horndean: Milestone Publications, 1987. A detailed, up-to-date study with many illustrations.

As with buses, so with trains; as well as the standard histories of the London Brighton and South Coast, London and South Western and Southern Railways, there are many books and articles written by and for enthusiasts dealing in some way with **railways** in our area; recent works by D. Fereday Glenn and Vic Mitchell and Keith Smith are always informative and well-illustrated. Two monographs are specific:

Course, Edwin, *Portsmouth Railways*, Portsmouth Papers No 6; Portsmouth: Portsmouth City Council, 1969. A well-documented historical summary.

Robertson, Kevin, *The Southsea Railway*, Southampton: Kingfisher Railway Productions, 1985. Eccentrically written and edited, but contains a wealth of research.

Finally, in considering public transport, the local **ferries** deserve a mention. Again, among several items, attention is drawn especially to:

Mackett, John, *The Portsmouth-Ryde Passage: a Personal View*, London: Ravensbourne Press. An illustrated history with glossary and bibliography.

Davies, R.K., *Solent Passages and their Steamers 1820-1981*, Newport: Isle of Wight County Press, 1982. Summary histories of the various passages with details of the vessels that operated them.

Childs, P.D., *The Gosport Ferry: the Centenary of the Portsmouth Harbour Ferry Company PLC 1883-1983: a Short History*, Gosport: Portsmouth Harbour Ferry Company, 1983. A very brief illustrated history by the company's chairman.

Burton, Lesley and Musslewhite, Brian, *Crossing the Harbour*, Horndean: Milestone Publications, 1987. A somewhat discursive account of the Portsmouth-Gosport crossing.

In addition to the items cited, most of which contain some pictures, there have been many general collections (of varying quality) of illustrations (also of varying quality) with captions (yet again of varying quality) of Portsmouth. In the last twenty years or so, the following are among those to have appeared:

Francis, David F., *Portsmouth Old and New*, Wakefield: EP Publishing, 1975. An album of views comparing scenes early in this century with the same view 1974-5.

Triggs, Anthony, *Portsmouth Past and Present*, Horndean: Milestone Publications, 1984. An imitation of the previous item.

Brown, Ron, *Portsmouth's Pictorial Past*, Horndean: Milestone Publications, 1985. A miscellaneous collection of old photographs with minimal but error-prone captions.

Francis, David and Rogers, Peter, *Portsmouth in Old Picture Postcards*, Zaltbommel: European Library, 1985. Contains 156 old views with copious captions.

McAvery, Ashley, *Southsea in Old Picture Postcards*, Zaltbommel: European Library, 1985. Contains 75 old views with captions.

(The commissioning editor of the publishers of the above two items was a little hazy in his geography! The Portsmouth volume contains many Southsea views! The Cosham volume cited below, concentrating on the northern part of the city, contains very little material duplicating the Portsmouth volume's content.)

Rogers, Peter N., *Cosham with Widley and Hilsea in Old Picture Postcards*, Zaltbommel: European Library, 1986. Contains 104 views with informative captions.

Triggs, Anthony, *Portsmouth Then and Now*, Horndean: Milestone Publications, 1986. [See note to his previous work, above.]

Rogers, Peter N. and Francis, David F., *Portsmouth in Old Photographs*, Gloucester: Alan Sutton, 1989. A thematic collection of old views.

Triggs, Anthony, *A Photographic History of Portsmouth: Fareham: Gosport: Havant: Horndean: Waterlooville*, Southampton: Ensign Publications, 1992. Inexplicably claims to be the first book of old photographs concentrating on Portsmouth, but it is of large format, the views are well reproduced, and by no means all have been published before.

Quail, Sarah and Stedman, John, *Images of Portsmouth*, Derby: Breedon Books, 1993. A thematic compilation, drawn from the collections at the Portsmouth City Records Office and Portsmouth City Museums. Captions and reproduction are of a uniformly high standard.

We have tried as far as possible in this volume to use items never, or only rarely, published before. We are indebted to Mr. F. Barter, Mr. K. Biles, the late Mr. B. Buckley, Mr. C. Collins, Mr. B. Gudge, Mr. A. Harris, Mr. D. Jordan, Mr. and Mrs. D. Miles, Mr. D. Sharp, Mr. T. Swetnam (formerly secretary/archivist of the Portsea Island Police Historical Society), Mr. D. Welch, *The Portsmouth News*, Portsmouth City Council and the Portsmouth City Records Office for making available and permitting the use of material from their collections, and for help in many and varied ways. A special 'thank you' is owed to Mr. B. Patterson for permitting the use of his maps as endpapers in this volume.

DAVID FRANCIS
PETER ROGERS

1. Mariners the world over will view the photograph with nostalgia, this being the first and last impression of 'Pompey' that sailors will retain on arriving at, or leaving port. For many seamen this was perhaps the last glimpse of home, in some cases for ever. The Round Tower in the picture has guarded the entrance to the harbour since *c*.1417 and in addition to its role as fortress has often provided a platform from which families could wave farewell or welcome home to their loved ones.

2. At the peak of their commercial success with shipbuilding the principal industry, Camber Docks are viewed at a time when Vospers provided employment for a workforce totalling several hundred. With the departure of the company the vacant sites were left ripe for sympathetic development, though at the time of writing little has been attempted to retain an atmosphere in keeping with the history and tradition of Old Portsmouth.

3.   This and the following picture were taken on 13 February 1895 and record scenes within the Camber Docks unlike any witnessed before or since. The movement of vessels within the confines of a small harbour was obviously made more difficult with sheet ice restricting many of the craft to their berths. The then lone chimney of the power station (opened in 1894) can be seen on the right.

4.   The buildings backing on to the dockside were in East Street. They included the *Orange Tree Tavern* (pictured) and the *Ellington*. Both hostelries closed in 1913.

5. Photographed in 1927, the original nature and atmosphere of the Camber Docks can be experienced in its traditional setting, with fishing craft lying at rest in the tiny harbour.

6. Old Portsmouth's Camber Docks are pictured in 1938. A small fishing port from the very earliest times, the Camber enjoyed considerable commercial expansion between the wars when massive quantities of coal and timber were unloaded in addition to the lesser cargoes transported to and from the harbour by coastal vessels.

7. The Camber's Town Quay later became the principal coaling wharf for Portsmouth and the entire local area. In the last years of the 19th century, however, scenes such as this would have been an almost daily part of life in Old Portsmouth when small coastal vessels like the *Thorney Island* would ply between local ports with cargoes of coal or timber.

8.  We are given a second chance to view the *Thorney Island*, this time under sail in Portsmouth Harbour, *c*.1894. With a most unusual configuration of sails, unlike any which would be seen today, she was built in Emsworth in 1871 (probably by J.D. Foster). The vessel is thought to be a flat-bottomed centreplate brigantine collier.

9.  Seaborne coal arriving at the Camber was off-loaded into reinforced storage bunkers by a system of overhead moving gantries. The bunker pictured here, 240 feet long and 97 feet wide, was capable of holding 15,000 tons of coal.

10. Photographs of the Portsmouth Town Gates have appeared in print many times but we are confident that this unique view of King George's Gate (also known as Quay Gate) will be new to most if not all of our readers. The massive proportions of this, the largest of the gates, can easily be realised and appreciated from this 'through' view.

11. An unusual feature still to be seen in Broad Street is the archway which once gave entry to the studio premises of W.H. Wyllie, the well known marine artist. The building itself was destroyed in the Blitz but the decorative arch remains; its unique incised inscription, 'Lat.30-47-25 North, Long.1-6-25 West', relates its actual position in the world!

12. With the Square Tower looming large on the left, the tantalising view is of pre-war Broad Street which until the bombing provided the visitor with a real flavour of Old Portsmouth. The family group are admiring the gilded bust of Charles I which has occupied a decorative niche in the wall since 1635.


13. The overhead tram wires suggest an earlier date than that of the previous picture; the scene however is again of Broad Street, this time at a different location. Whilst most of the left-hand buildings remain intact, those on the right were totally destroyed during the air raids on Portsmouth.

14.　Photographs taken in the last years of the 19th century, and recently re-discovered in a family album, have given a new perspective to our present-day Broad Street. The date of this and the following pictures is 28 August 1894 and included among the 'top brass' is Prince Arthur, Duke of Connaught. The party is about to pass Bathing Lane.

15.　The reason for the presence of the Royal Party becomes apparent when we determine that a military exercise is to take place on the Browndown Ranges at Gosport and that the soldiers and weaponry are waiting to board the floating bridge. The men are believed to be of the Hampshire Regiment and the shadows indicate that it is early morning.

16. Returning from the Gosport shores, the soldiers and horses will look forward to a well earned rest in the comfort of the barracks.

17. While the military hardwear is being dis-embarked, the trades vehicles on the left of the picture are waiting to board the ferry. The terrace in each of these photographs can be compared with the Broad Street of 1994 and shows surprisingly little change from 1894, save for the fact that where once could be found four pubs, today there are none!

18.  High tides still occasionally cause flooding in Broad Street though perhaps less frequently than of old. The photograph was taken in the 1890s by Herbert Bailey, chemist, whose premises at number 70 are seen in the picture; he is also credited with having produced the other period photographs of Broad Street and Camber Docks in this volume.

19.  The memorial, once a feature of Old Portsmouth's Grand Parade, was erected as a tribute to those members of the 8th King's Regiment who lost their lives in the Indian Mutiny 1857/59. The Garrison Church provides the background.

20. With the Garrison Church out of sight to the left, the view is of Grand Parade, Old Portsmouth in the last years of the 19th century. The Long Curtain fortifications are still under military control at this time with no promenade on the seaward side. Archaeological exploration of the parade in 1976 revealed evidence of an ancient tunnel beneath the surface.

21. Sir Bernard de Gomme's massive defence system constructed around Portsmouth c.1687 was almost entirely removed in the last quarter of the 19th century. Of the meagre photographic evidence which is left to us, this picture perhaps illustrates best the extent of those defensive works. Viewed across the moats and ramparts are seen, on the left, the *Royal Pier Hotel* (now Rees Hall) and on the right *The Queens Hotel*.

22. Born in Blackheath in 1834, Sarah Robinson developed acute spinal curvature while still a child, a handicap which confined her to a steel support for the remainder of her long life (she died in 1921). Determined to spread Christian moral values, particularly among servicemen, she sought to establish soldiers' and sailors' institutes in naval and garrison towns.

23. Suitable premises were built or purchased in Portsmouth, Portsea and Landport, the *Speedwell Hotel* in Commercial Road and the old *Fountain Inn* in the High Street offering the greater accommodation. This photograph is of the *Fountain Inn* following its conversion.

24.   Photographed from gardens at the rear, Sarah Robinson's High Street premises can now be judged for the extraordinary size and scope of accommodation which they afforded her.

25.   The success of Miss Robinson's campaign was acknowledged when hard-living, hard-drinking men were converted to a Christian, Temperance way of life as a result of attending her lectures and reading the scriptures. In this photograph of 1876, a Bible class comprises Royal Marines and one sailor.

26. Sarah Robinson's 'Helping Hand Temperance Society' admitted wives of servicemen into its Civilian Branch and on this very decorative, colourful certificate of membership it will be noted that Maria Rimmington (wife of the Royal Marine groom pictured elsewhere in this volume) has been admitted into the society, having 'signed the pledge' in 1885.

27. The officer classes were later included in Miss Robinson's plans and, as finance became available, premises were leased or purchased to extend her good works. The buildings seen here are located in Penny Street and Grand Parade.

28. The Y.M.C.A. premises which had earlier been the *Fountain Inn* and, later, Sarah Robinson's Hostel, can be noted on the right of this pre-war photograph of the High Street, Old Portsmouth. Having survived the bombing, the building was demolished in the post-war years, an apartment block taking its place.

29. This photograph of Oyster Street, Old Portsmouth, was recorded in the mid-1930s. Possibly the oldest inhabited part of the town, its origins date from at least the 12th century.

30. Oyster Street is pictured again following the bombing raids of 1940. When these properties, many of which were centuries old, were cleared away, an extensive archaeological examination of the site revealed considerable evidence of continued occupation for at least 700 years; quantities of worked flint from the Neolithic to the early Bronze Age (2500-1500 B.C.) also attest to the seasonal occupation of our ancient itinerant ancestors. Reproduced with the permission of *The Portsmouth News*.

31. In the 1890s, Nobb's Lane in Old Portsmouth was condemned by Sarah Robinson as a base for the town's most evil prostitutes: 'The wretched women are bolder than anywhere else. They seem older and uglier and more experienced. I saw and heard more disgusting things than I ever before encountered at Aldershot ...'. It was from such an environment that Sarah wished to protect servicemen and their families.

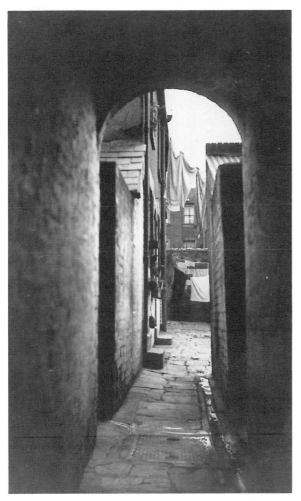

32. Ayott's Court, pictured here, was one of many similarly-styled groups of dwellings originating from the Georgian period or earlier. Providing a far from decent living standard they survived for the most part until the bombing of the Second World War. The court was a close neighbour of Nobb's Lane, both being located off Warblington Street.

33. A worthy son of Portsmouth, John Pounds, severely disabled in a dockyard accident, earned a meagre living repairing boots at his tiny home. This dauntless and most charitable of men also took upon himself the task of educating local street urchins, often sharing a meal with them in his one downstairs room. He died in 1839, his home remaining as a memorial until 1939.

34.  In 1928 Major Douglas Sharp took over these premises in High Street from the Southern Cross Motor Company and traded successfully as the United Service Garage until the bombing of the Second World War destroyed almost all of this section of the street, including the Unitarian Church next door and the old Shakespearean theatre (not pictured). This photograph is dated 1936.

35.  The garage and workshops of the previous photograph could also be accessed from nearby St Thomas's Street and here we see the staff together with motor cars of the period. The large building next door was, at this time, Smithers Pickle Factory from where noxious odours would issue to contaminate the district! The photograph is dated 1928.

36.  One-time residence of the Lieutenant Governor of Portsmouth, this fine building which once graced the High Street is seen at the time of the Diamond Jubilee of Her Majesty Queen Victoria.

37.  Portsea Hard, c.1910, seen from the causeway giving access to the Harbour station and ferries. The Hard provides a fine array of 18th- and 19th-century buildings, almost all of them pubs or refreshment houses. The view from the same spot today would be interrupted by the transport interchange.

38. (*left*) Typical of the congested areas of Portsea was Pay's Buildings; tiny artisan dwellings located in a court crammed between the equally overcrowded and suffocating side streets. The sharing of communal WCs and the total lack of garden space placed such properties high on the council list of pre-war redevelopment.

39. (*below right*) Mutinous naval riots within Portsmouth's Royal Naval Barracks in 1906 prompted the authorities to screen the railings seen here with corrugated iron sheeting, thus preventing both ratings and public from exchanging any form of communication which might further aggravate a repeat of the incident. It was not until 1957 that a more enlightened Commodore Thompson obtained permission for the removal of the iron cladding.

40. (*bottom*) At midday on 12 August 1940 a force of Ju88 German bombers, comprising at least 70 aircraft, made a concerted attack on the Dockyard and Portsea. Considerable damage was experienced including that seen here in Edinburgh Road when both the Royal Naval Officers' Mess and Barracks were hit; at the same time, a section of railings (the subject of the previous photograph), was destroyed. Reproduced with the permission of *The Portsmouth News*.

41.  H.M.S. *Dreadnought*, the first in a class of revolutionary battleship design, was launched in Portsmouth on Saturday 10 February 1906 by His Majesty King Edward. All records were beaten in her construction. She was launched only five months after being on the stocks and was commissioned just one year after her first keel plates were laid.

42. Portsmouth Dockyard for centuries had been the centre of naval shipbuilding in Britain and, following the successful completion of *Dreadnought*, continued the tradition until the last vessel to leave the slipway, H.M.S. *Andromeda*, a frigate of the *Leander* class, was launched in 1968. Our picture shows H.M.S. *Dreadnought* surrounded by attendant vessels shortly after becoming waterborne.

43.  Lord Tredegar's steam yacht *Liberty* is pictured at Portsmouth following conversion for work as a hospital ship. Lord Tredegar bore the entire cost of the work and took command himself having been granted by the Admiralty a commission as lieutenant in the R.N.R. The *Liberty* was white with a broad red band, and a large red cross painted amidships.

44.  Naval disasters have always affected those families whose menfolk crewed Portsmouth ships. Such was the case on 25 April 1908 when H.M.S. *Gladiator* was in collision with the Atlantic liner S.S. *St Paul* off Yarmouth in the Isle of Wight. This tragedy claimed the lives of 27 crew members. Lying in shallow water not too distant from the shore, the wreck quickly became an attraction for morbid sensation seekers who, incidentally, provided an additional source of revenue for boat owners happy to ply for hire.

**GLADIATOR'S TERRIBLE INJURIES REVEALED.**

THE GREAT RENT, SHOWING THAT THE ST. PAUL STRUCK THE CRUISER A SLANTING BLOW. D.—Port got hole in the Gladiator's side. A.—Point at which the St. Paul struck. B.—Deep hole made by St. Paul at the end of the contact. C.—Collision mat which the Gladiator's crew tried to place in position before the ship foundered.

45.   Following a difficult salvage operation, H.M.S. *Gladiator* was docked at Portsmouth where the extent of her damage was revealed.

46.   Meanwhile, a Southampton dry dock provided repair facilities for the S.S. *St Paul*.

47.   The last of the Mosquito class of destroyers, H.M.S. *Coquette* was involved in this unfortunate incident in Portsmouth Harbour on 3 May 1907. A news report which followed the mishap suggested that she lost control on the way out of harbour, took an erratic turn and headed at 15 knots for the coaling depot! With crushed bows she was taken alongside and later docked for repair.

48.   Following a collision with the S.S. *Transporter* on 3 September 1909, the paddle steamer *Duchess of Kent* was beached alongside the Saluting Platform in Old Portsmouth where a large crowd gathered to view the damage. Successfully disembarking 400 passengers, the vessel was later patched sufficiently well to allow her to proceed (surprisingly under her own steam) to Southampton.

49. In September 1870 the town of Portsmouth was plunged into mourning when learning of the loss of H.M.S. *Captain* in the Bay of Biscay. In one Portsea street alone it was recorded that 30 wives had been widowed. Of a crew of 600, only 18 seamen survived. This very early photograph pictures those survivors, still in a ragged state on their return to Portsmouth.

51. Haslar's Royal Naval Cemetery became the final resting place of seamen who had died on shore or whose bodies were recovered from the sea or ships on which they had served. A ship's anchor recovered from H.M.S. *Eurydice* surmounts this impressive memorial which records the names of all those lost in the tragedy of 1878.

50. Portsmouth is accustomed to disaster; no 'Pompey' vessel has ever gone down in war or peace without causing bereavement to many Portsmouth families. Perhaps the greatest 19th-century tragedy to affect local folk was the inexplicable loss of H.M.S. *Eurydice* which foundered in a 10-minute squall off Ventnor in the Isle of Wight in March 1878 on her way home from the West Indies. The two seamen pictured here, Fletcher and Cuddiford, were the only survivors from an estimated 400 men.

52.   Familiar to generations of seamen and dockyard workers, the King's Stairs were the traditional point of arrival or departure for Royalty or Heads of State. In a modern world, however, such comings and goings are usually catered for by methods which include covered ships' gangways or helicopter landings!

53.   Displaying the big guns of H.M.S. *Royal Sovereign*, the picture also reveals South Railway Jetty and the covered concourse built to receive members of the Monarchy who would arrive here on the Royal Train.

54.   A scene typical of Portsmouth Harbour in 1907.

55.   A torpedo boat is pictured undergoing repairs while in dry dock. In the early years of this century, commercial photographers seem to have had little if any restriction placed upon their activities whilst recording scenes within the dockyard. Cameras would not now be permitted in areas of sensitive security such as are depicted in these picture postcards.

56. Prior to the First World War the sense of national security was seemingly non-existent, as is confirmed by the vast numbers of photographs recording locations which, even then, would have been invaluable to a hostile foreign power. The semaphore tower (pictured here *c.*1907) was destroyed by fire in December 1913 due, it has been claimed, to the activities of a German espionage cell.

57. Readers who recall the extensive use of barrage balloons in war-time Portsmouth probably remain unaware of the fact that this form of defence against low flying aircraft was also used by shipping in both world wars. Photographed in the Solent, this craft is seen with its balloon tethered in a passive role awaiting a possible emergency when it would be raised aloft to a combatant height.

58. An almost 'posed' situation enabled a very shrewd photographer to obtain this unique picture of H.M.S. *Nelson* passing the memorial anchor from Admiral Lord Nelson's H.M.S. *Victory*, *c.*1930.

59. Locally-based Young's Brewery having supplied the ale, these Royal Marines, dressed in the authentic uniforms of 1805, are seen 'splicing the mainbrace' alongside H.M.S. *Victory* on a naval occasion prior to the Second World War.

60.  Portsmouth Dockyard fire station is graphically presented in this remarkable commercial postcard of 1904. The card is just one of a series depicting the life and times of the establishment in the early years of the century. Both security and fire fighting duties were at that time provided by the Metropolitan Police Force in each of the Royal Dockyards.

61. Many events have been staged in the Victory Arena since the old vessel was dry-berthed in 1922; however, the reason for this gathering of superb old motor cars is not known; suffice to say that it was sufficiently important to bring that most prolific of local photographers, Stephen Cribb, to record the scene!

62. The 1906 families' day at H.M.S. *Excellent*, Whale Island, demonstrates that no effort was spared in providing amusements to entertain and thrill the youngsters. The naval method of transferring men, ship to ship by 'jackstay', is put to good use with this aerial ride in a canvas 'bucket'.

63.  Many clues can be discovered in this photograph to determine the era in which it was recorded. The fact that a tramcar is visible, entering the Guildhall Square from the right, suggests that it must be prior to 1937 (the last vehicle ran on 10 November 1936). The picture also includes a great number of pre-war landmarks which will generate interest among local historians.

64. The Guildhall Square is seen before pedestrianisation. Much of the area beyond this view was destroyed in the bombing raids on Portsmouth, although Russell Street was making a brave show with most of its shops still trading. (Photograph copyright Portsmouth City Council.)

65. A second aerial view shows the Guildhall area before the square was closed to traffic, but with the war damage cleared away. In the foreground, left to right, may be seen the old swimming baths (with its successor already in place on the other side of the railway), the flattened site of St Michael's Church, the orphanage, and St Andrew's Presbyterian Church. New roads and University buildings have since substantially altered the geography of the area. (Photograph copyright Portsmouth City Council.)

Labourhouse & Stores
Salem Chapel
Racquet Court
Penitentiary whits Garden
Colonel of Artillery
Pond
Russell St
Greetham St
Timber Yard
Salem St
White Swan St
Park View
Landport Road to Portsmouth

66.   Dating from *c*.1850, this most interesting sketch reveals the road from the railway station in a southerly direction. The Town Hall has yet to be built on a site occupied by the Colonel of Artillery; a racquets court is a precursor to the Theatre Royal. Also noted are Greetham Street, Russell Street, Landport Road (to Old Portsmouth), Salem Street and Salem Church, Tollervy's pond, timber yard, Park View, *White Swan* and, surprisingly, a penitentiary!

67.   In this interesting bird's-eye view of central Portsmouth it is possible to recognise properties which remain today in close proximity to those which were blitzed or were otherwise removed. There is a glimpse of the Empire Palace Music Hall, Trafalgar Institute, Madden's restaurant, *Evening News* Offices, Connaught Drill Hall and Sarah Robinson's 'Sailor's Welcome', where a roof sign warns 'PREPARE TO MEET THY GOD', while another on the wall simply says 'WELCOME'!

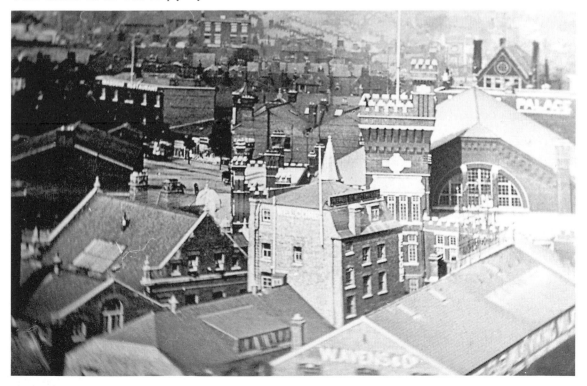

69. (*above*) A further photographic rarity, this time the Empire Palace Music Hall in 1897, again with decorations celebrating Queen Victoria's Jubilee. Opened in 1891 and traditional in the true sense of music hall (drinks could be consumed whilst watching the performance from the promenade bar), the theatre underwent refurbishment and a name change in 1913 when it became the 'Coliseum Theatre'. The name reverted to 'The Empire' in 1950 and the building was demolished in 1958.

68. (*above*) Devotees of the Theatre Royal and local historians alike will no doubt delight in this particularly rare photograph of 1897. Decorative tributes in celebration of Queen Victoria's Diamond Jubilee festoon the façade of the building. Of particular interest to the theatrical historian, however, are the obvious alterations which have been made to the portico and colonnade of 1874 compared with that of 1884 and the present construction of 1900.

70. (*right*) Open displays of fish, game and poultry, together with street pollution of the period, were commonplace before the awareness of the need for hygiene. The Landport (Commercial Road) premises of Jas. Patterson can be identified once more in the following picture.

71.   An earlier name for Landport had been 'Halfway Houses' and, in this 1912 picture postcard, what were the last of those properties can be seen on the left of the picture. Adjacent to the horse-drawn cart may be noticed the first of the Timothy White retail premises, *The Bakers' Arms* and the premises of Jas. Patterson, fishmonger.

72.   In an inflationary world, a natural progression from an original Penny Bazaar to a 'Penny & Sixpenny' store possibly laid the foundations for the Marks & Spencer success story. The original Portsmouth store, seen here in Commercial Road *c.*1910, was but a few yards from their present modern departmental premises.

73. (*left*) A rare photograph of the Dickens birthplace; there is no visible clue that this is indeed the location of his birth. In the early years after the Borough acquired the property there was, in fact, a tablet set in the pavement outside the house. Even this had been against the wishes of the author who had inserted a clause in his will preventing the erection of any conspicuous memorial to him.

74. (*below left*) An early curator of the Dickens Birthplace Museum was Mr. Alfred A. Seale. What amounts to a glowing testimonial appears on the reverse of his photograph where, among other attributes, he is credited with having an outstanding knowledge of Dickens and is claimed to be the greatest living authority on the man and the subject.

75. (*below*) Recorded *c*.1930, the picture is self-explanatory; costumed in dress of the period, the merrymakers are gathered at an annual celebration of the birth of Charles Dickens.

76.   Church Path North at Landport provided access to many lesser streets of which George's Place was one. In this view recorded in the mid '30s the photographer, like the Pied Piper, has attracted the interest of local children. An adjoining street was Alice Place and one must pose the question, who were George and Alice?

77.   Chance Street, Landport is pictured in more or less festive mood for the Silver Jubilee of 1935. A notice on the wall advises that the district is due for demolition under the 1930 Slum Clearance Act. Much of Portsea had by this time been subjected to clearance and soon it was to be the turn of Landport.

78. The clearance which took take place in Chance Street was actually perpetrated by a lone German aircraft on the evening of 23 December 1940. A single huge explosion, which has never been satisfactorily explained, destroyed at least 15 streets. The incident, which has no parallel, has since become known as the Conway Street disaster. (Reproduced with the permission of *The Portsmouth News*.)

79. Jubilee Terrace was one of the earliest of Southsea's Regency terraces, having been completed by 1815. By the time of this photograph (around 1900), it was already in decline as a fashionable residential area, although the Turkish Baths survived until 1936.

80. The southern end of Palmerston Road. Southsea first developed as a residential suburb for naval officers (retired and active) and other military personnel. Palmerston Road became the hub of this fashionable area, known locally as 'the village'. Note the 'bath' chairs and the apparently haphazard rule of the road then applying!

81. In 1924, with just £100 borrowed from a close relative, Major Douglas Sharp ventured into the motor trade. With the barest of workshop facilities in Auckland Road, his first showroom was opened 10 years later in 1934 on the corner of Auckland and Palmerston Roads, Southsea. (The premises also appear in a different guise in the previous photograph.)

82. 1935 saw the company (United Service Garages) appointed as Vauxhall Distributors for South Hampshire and West Sussex. Innovative methods of advertising prompted Major Sharp to engage well-known personalities in the promotion of the Vauxhall range of vehicles; here we see boxer Jack Doyle and film star Judith Allen with Vauxhall's Scoota-car.

83. Theatre-goers of the 1930s and '40s will recall Teddy Brown, the overweight but talented xylophonist; it is not recorded whether on this occasion he attempted to ease his ample 27 stone into the miniature vehicle! Major Douglas Sharp can be seen on the right of the photograph which is dated 1936.

WESTERN Bros.
KENNETH & George    These Radio Cads

IVOR
MORETON  DAVE
KAYE

Radio's Rhythm Maniacs    The Wizard of
the Drums.

OSSIE NOBLE

NORMAN CARROLL  Comedian

HYLDA BAKER  Comedienne

HARVARD, MORTIMER & KENDRICK

WATSON  A North Country
Comic

STAGE DOOR

CPO 359

84.   The last of these promotional photographs features 'Kenneth & George' (the Western Brothers). Two voices with one piano, they were a popular act on the music halls and the radio. Admiring a Vauxhall 25 HP Saloon, they are photographed outside the Hippodrome Theatre in 1936.

85. Three views of the popular Handley's Corner and Palmerston Road, Southsea. The first photograph shows the mass of decorations displayed to welcome the men of the French Fleet who visited the town in the spirit of 'Entente Cordiale' in 1905.

86. The major blitz of 10 January 1941 destroyed all the buildings seen in the previous picture. Handley's department store is now a twisted, ugly mass of steel and masonry. In this one raid, each of Portsmouth's principal shopping centres was obliterated; Commercial Road, Kings Road and Palmerston Road. (Reproduced with the permission of *The Portsmouth News*.)

87. (*top left*) When time and manpower allowed, the city's bombed sites were cleared of debris and in some cases small garden areas were created in an attempt both to relieve and disguise the scars left by the air raids. The scene was photographed at Handley's Corner, at the junction of Palmerston, Osborne and Portland Roads.

88. (*above*) Pictured in 1900, the scene is totally unrecognisable today. The photograph presents no clues as to location other than the printed title. Elm Grove, taking its name from the avenue of trees, was at this time home to the wealthy Southsea aristocracy; grand houses in spacious grounds have long been replaced or converted to create one of the town's major shopping venues.

89. (*left*) A guide book of 1911 describes Grove Road as 'perhaps the most shady and rural in Southsea'. The scene here is one of pre-First World War tranquillity. A retired colonel resided in Oak Cottage, and the Reverend and Mrs. Reed operated a ladies' academy next door.

BRANKSMERE
HOSPITAL
SOUTHSEA
S. CRIBB PHOTO.

90. During the First World War, as a family gesture to Portsmouth's war effort, Sir Rupert Brickwood allowed his house, Branksmere, sited in Southsea on the corner of Kent Road and Queen's Crescent, to be used as a Red Cross Hospital.

91.   At a charity fête and bazaar held at Branksmere in July 1917, the proceedings were opened by the Marchioness of Winchester.

92.   Whilst tea on the lawn was being served with the usual grace and decorum by uniformed nurses, military patients who were obviously 'on the mend' were staging a mini regatta on the ornamental lake to the possible consternation of the Matron.

93.   Shortly following the First World War, Branksmere experienced a change of name and ownership when it became Byculla, an independent residential school for the daughters of gentlemen and, although times and circumstances have changed, the tradition of tea on the lawn remains an English institution. On this occasion parents are enjoying tea at the annual speech and prize day.


94.   An interior view of Byculla shows the Sixth Form sitting room with a door opening into the hall. (This description is given on the reverse of the picture, sent by a young lady pupil to her parents.)

95.   Albert Road, Southsea, photographed after the introduction of electric tramcars in 1901 yet prior to the opening of the Kings Theatre in 1907. The future of Portsmouth's oldest existing police station (built 1872) is now in doubt; having long outlived its usefulness it is now closed, awaiting possible development of the site.

96.   Designed by doyen of Edwardian theatre architects, Frank Matcham, Southsea's Kings Theatre opened in 1907. The Primitive Methodist Church, near neighbour of the Kings, was later converted into the Apollo Cinema, a move which prompted the Kings itself to take on the role of cinema in order to cope with the increasing loss of theatre audiences to the silver screen.

97.   Unruly audiences were discouraged by the sign displayed in the upper gallery ('The Gods'); 'Whistling and shouting strictly prohibited. Offenders will be ejected'!

98.   Henry Brodribb Irving, son of Sir Henry Irving, opened in the Kings first productions of *The Lyons Mail*, *The Bells* and his costumed role, *Charles the First*.

99. The peace and tranquillity of Southsea's Chelsea Road in 1906 contrasts sharply with the scene recorded in the following photograph.

100. Portsmouth experienced its third bombing raid on 24 August 1940 when 40 German aircraft devastated the city with 67 bombs. Chelsea Road sustained the damage recorded here. This attack on the city was responsible for the deaths of 125 persons with an additional 300 wounded. (Reproduced with the permission of *The Portsmouth News*.)

101. Fawcett Road *c*.1910 displays shop fronts almost identical to those of the present day. Gone, however, are the tramlines and overhead wires and booms. The elegance of those years is also lost to us; note for example the decorative ironwork on booms, supporting poles and lamp post when compared with the featureless, soulless street furniture of today.

102.   An early Clarence Pier shares this view with the King's Rooms and an, as yet, unmetalled promenade and seafront road. The year is 1888. Lord Frederick Fitzclarence had been responsible for creating both promenade and road in 1848; it was, however, the Borough Engineer Percy Boulnois who upgraded the works to something approaching our present standard in the last years of the 19th century.

103.   This view at the western end of Clarence Esplanade shows the entrance to Clarence Pier (on the left), and the frontage of the *Esplanade Hotel*. The hotel had been converted in 1877 from the former King's Rooms, built originally in 1816 as a pump room, baths and reading room. The hotel was constructed entirely of wood and plaster to facilitate rapid demolition in case the nearby shore batteries ever needed to fire across the site.

104. A particularly fine aerial view of Clarence Pier also reveals much of pre-war Southsea, for example, St Paul's Church and Hambrook Brewery in addition to the massive complex that was Victoria, Cambridge and Clarence Barracks. Originally built in 1861, the pier was then of lesser proportions, providing only a simple landing stage for the Isle of Wight steamers.

105. Improved and enlarged, the pier deck housed the ornate pavilion (1882) and a funfair, as well as providing facilities for skating and promenading in addition to increased berthing for passenger ferries. A horse tramway conveyed passengers to and from Portsmouth Town railway station across the pier deck.

106. A 1930s widening of the promenade considerably reduced this area of beach, so depriving many local folk of the attractions of sun and sea bathing.

107. There were, of course, occasions when the seashore was placed out of bounds by the vagaries of the weather!

108.  A carnival atmosphere is apparent in this seaside view of 1907. The use of a strong magnifying glass will reveal that this is indeed Regatta Day and that vendors of all kinds are doing their best to attract the crowds. One hopes that all was dispersed before the return of high water.

109. Developed from a veritable wasteland, Southsea's Children's Corner very soon proved its worth. Caring parents are seen shepherding their offspring in the queue awaiting to mount the steps of the slide whilst onlookers watch the family fun from a vantage point on the promenade.

110. 1930 saw the completion of Children's Corner at Southsea. Attractions included the boating pool, paddling and swimming pools and also the very popular miniature railway. The canoes and paddle craft seen here were later augmented with the quaintly named 'Pop Pop' boats powered by paraffin engines which, of no great speed, were considered to be safe even when handled by children.

111.  The principal attraction at Children's Corner was undoubtedly the steam railway. Miniature engineering at its finest, the trains had an immense 'pulling power' in both locomotion and public interest, adults as well as children being drawn to admire the mechanics of the pygmy engines.

112.  Scenes such as this at Southsea were commonplace on each of the sovereign's birthdays with troops from the Garrison parading as a token of loyalty to the Monarch. The year is 1888.

113. Empire Day was once celebrated nationwide on the anniversary of Queen Victoria's birthday and, each year, parades and demonstrations of loyalty were eagerly looked forward to and participated in by school children, youth groups, public employees and military alike. This scene recorded in 1911 depicts a horse-drawn Britannia heading a column of uniformed scouts and naval cadets across Southsea Common.

114. A pre-war aerial view of Clarence Parade and Lennox Road also shows (top centre) the tiny Clarendon Park, facing an indoor skating rink which was later to become the premises of a major garage company. The greenhouses and nurseries of E. & E. Smee, local florists, dominate the photograph top right.

115. Built as a result of private enterprise, the first South Parade Pier was opened on 26 July 1879 by Princess Edward of Saxe Weimar, wife of Portsmouth's Lieutenant Governor. Rapidly becoming a popular venue for both leisure and pleasurable entertainment, the pier filled a need as a social outlet in the growing district of Southsea until 1904 when it was sadly destroyed by fire on the afternoon of 19 July.

116. Crowds of spectators soon gathered to witness the spectacle and it can also be noted that Royal Marines in 'undress' uniform were enlisted (with rifles at the ready) to prevent the public from causing any hindrance to the fire crews.

117. Two years after the fire, the derelict structure was demolished and removed for its new owners Portsmouth Corporation. Our picture shows workmen who were employed in building the second pier which, at a cost of £70,000, opened in 1908.

118.  In the early years of its existence the new pier became known as 'The White Lady', a name coined because of the attractive design and pristine white and silver appearance which made it the showpiece of Southsea.

119.  At the outbreak of the Second World War, the connecting deck linking the two halves of the pier, in keeping with seaside piers elsewhere, was removed, so creating an obstacle to a potential invading enemy. This aerial view also reveals parts of Southsea which include, top left of centre, the old East Southsea railway station buildings.

120.   Limitations imposed by the lack of today's modern transport failed to deter the intrepid photographer who somehow always managed to attend events and disasters of this nature. Luckily for the hotel proprietors, the fire damage was confined to the upper storeys of the building and there were no reports of injury or death.

121.   Converted from a marshy wasteland where wildfowl were the only visitors, the Canoe Lake was created in 1886 by the Borough Engineer, Percy H. Boulnois. This dedicated and far-sighted man gave to Southsea one of its greatest assets for, year in year out, the lake and surrounding gardens attract more visitors than perhaps any other local amenity.

122.   Each year, Southsea stages a tennis tournament which has deservedly become a mecca for the finest amateur and county players in the country. This scene was recorded at the Canoe Lake tennis courts in 1914. Whilst the serious contenders were competing for trophies on the courts (top right of this picture), less dedicated players enjoyed less competitive tennis on the nearby public courts.

123. Beaches at Clarence and Southsea had long provided seasonal amenities for the public—refreshments, shops, changing cubicles and so on and, in an attempt to promote and popularise the neglected Eastney beach, the city provided tents and deck chairs for hire in the '30s. The Royal Marines' swimming pool and the butts on the firing ranges are seen in the background.

124.  The groom pictured here with the Royal Marine Adjutant of Eastney Barracks, *c*.1888, is Alfred Rimmington. Born in Lincolnshire in 1847, he walked the 40 miles to Sheffield where he enlisted in the Royal Marines in 1867 prior to joining the regiment at Portsmouth. Following his discharge to pension he continued his service to the corps as resident groom.

125.  The cottages pictured were on land owned by James Goldsmith and, indeed, were also probably his property. It is possible to relate to the location today; the arched windows on the right were at the rear of the Congregational Chapel which later became Milton's first Public Library.

126. Remarkable if only for its age, this is the earliest known photograph of a Portsmouth Borough Policeman. Dated 1853 the portrait is of P.C. 31 George Softly.

127. The only surviving photograph of the Borough Force taken in 1862, also reveals the first purpose-built police station in the town. Sited near Tollervy's pond, it occupied a location which is today roughly that of the City's Central Library in the Guildhall Square.

128. Mounted officers of the Portsmouth Borough Police are pictured in Edinburgh Road on 11 June 1909 awaiting the arrival of the Duchess of Albany who, on that date, opened the services' home which bore her name.

129.   This photograph features the Portsmouth Police Band in July 1912.
It is interesting to note the varying styles of uniform dress tunics of
constables, sergeants and officers, and also the cap badges displaying the
lyre motif, any one of which would be a collector's 'prize' today.

130. En route to the Portsmouth Power Station, *c.*1922, is the new 5000W Metropolitan Vickers Generator which was installed in that year. Lion Terrace (pictured) was, at that time, one of the few locations spacious enough to have been used as an assembly point in an otherwise congested part of town. It is likely that abnormal loads would habitually rendez-vous here whilst awaiting clearance to proceed to their destination in Old Portsmouth.

131. One can imagine the problems encountered when manoeuvring and off-loading heavy equipment at the Power Station which was then sited in the confined backstreets of Old Portsmouth.

132. This advertisement, dated 1925, complements the accompanying photograph taken in the same year. The 'charabanc' booking kiosks, together with the vehicles, have occupied the same prominent seafront location for upwards of 70 years.

## SOUTHSEA TOURIST CO. LTD.

### The GREY CARS with the Highest Reputation.

*COMFORT*

*RELIABILITY*

*Open Coach.*

TRAVEL BY THE ALL WEATHER DE-LUXE CARS.
DAY and HALF-DAY TOURS to all Places of Interest. Starting from SOUTH PARADE PIER.

## Tours in the Isle of Wight
FARE INCLUDES BOAT JOURNEY AND ALL PIER TOLLS
HOTEL AND BOARDING HOUSE PARTIES SPECIALLY CATERED FOR.

*All Seats may be booked in advance at the Offices at:—*

49 Middle Street      South Parade Pier
53 Clarendon Road   North End Junction

P H O N E

2 2 3 1

*Converted to Closed Saloon in few minutes.*

DAILY SERVICES TO AND FROM LONDON DURING THE SEASON

# MOTOR COACH TOURS

133. Photograph to accompany advertisement.

134.  Each and every royal and civic occasion prompted the Portsmouth Public Transport Department to decorate extensively one of its passenger vehicles, be it tramcar or trolley bus. The event recorded here is the Silver Jubilee of His Majesty King George V and Queen Mary in 1935.

135.  The Milton Extension via Goldsmith Avenue was opened on 20 July 1909 with the inaugural tramcar carrying members of the Tramways Committee together with representatives of the Corporation. It was reported that a particularly comfortable ride was experienced due to the innovative use of welded track joints.

136.  Continued expansion of Portsmouth's tramway system involved track-laying at the junction of Festing Road and Highland Road. Beyond the fence and running beneath the road to the left was the line of the railway which ran from Fratton to East Southsea station. The photograph was taken during the summer of 1913.

137.  Tramway track-laying in Twyford Avenue. Pictured is the scene outside the *Mother Shipton* public house where there is a double track converging into interlaced track in the direction of the nearby terminus. The year is 1913.

138. Where Commercial Road dipped below the high level railway platform, surface water would sometimes present a hazard to traffic. Here, to the obvious amusement of passers-by, tramcar number 91 carefully makes its way south, en route to Clarence Pier.

139. A Portsmouth Corporation (C.P.P.T.D.) 'closed top' tramcar of innovative design is pictured at the 'stub and loop' Clarence Pier Terminus in 1933. Following behind is a tramcar belonging to the Portsdown & Horndean Light Railway Company which, in 1925, had negotiated joint use of this line.

140. Bearing the caption 'Scouts Day, 14 Feb.', this 1910 picture postcard (dated 3 March of that year) reveals a conflict in dates in that 'Founders Day' of the scouting movement is 21 February. With not a boy scout in sight, there may of course be yet another explanation of Scouts' Day. The cavalcade is seen crossing Southsea Common.

141. Borough police stations invariably incorporated a garage to accommodate one fire appliance. This photograph, however, is of the police fire brigade, crew and engine outside the brigade headquarters in Park Road.

142. Portsmouth's new gaol was opened at Kingston in 1877. A uniformed police driver has the unenviable task of transporting miscreants through the local streets in the 'Black Maria' police van seen here.

143.   Here is a nostalgic view of Fratton Bridge looking along Goldsmith Avenue. Many readers will remember the *Crystal Palace* pub, managed for many years by ex-Pompey footballer Jock Anderson. The Royal British Legion building to the left was once a cinema, the Fratton Electric Theatre. These words appeared in mosaic on the floor of the entrance area, and are still preserved under the re-arranged road which now covers the site. (Photograph copyright Portsmouth City Council.)

144.   Just to the right of the previous view, the scene, at least in the foreground, has changed markedly with the demolition of the insurance building and the construction of a roundabout. The Riley car would have been something of a collector's item even at the date of the photograph *c*.1957. (Photograph copyright Portsmouth City Council.)

145.  'A year of great enterprise, Portsmouth's successful adventure', were words used at the opening of the City Airport in July 1932.  Air circuses, private flying, chartered flights and joy riding became a novel and attractive past-time for the many spectators who were drawn to this new form of local entertainment.

146.  Great Salterns, a centuries-old wasteland of tidal marshes and scrub, had been partially reclaimed to form the city's first municipal golf course which was declared open on 14 July 1926.  Six years later, the airport became a close neighbour, as this photograph suggests.

147. What is presumably a circus parade is travelling northwards along Fratton Road towards Kingston Cross. *The Tramway Arms*, just discernible in the left background, then stood at the junction of Lake Road and Fratton Road. The former has subsequently been re-aligned further south, more or less immediately to the left of the photographer who recorded the scene.

148. Photographed on a date sometime prior to 1910, the scene is that of Kingston Cross where London Road and Kingston Road meet with Kingston Crescent. The tram is southbound and turning right.

149.   On 11 July 1940 Portsmouth experienced its first ever bombing raid when, at 6 p.m. precisely, German raiders attacked targets within the Dockyard and Portsmouth Harbour. The greatest damage, however, was caused to civilian property at Rudmore, North End and Kingston. Deaths among first-aid workers at Drayton Road School were the first recorded in wartime Portsmouth. The raid also destroyed the *Blue Anchor* pub at Kingston Cross, which is the subject of this photograph. (Reproduced with the permission of *The Portsmouth News*.)

150.   The residential appearance of London Road in 1906 is broken by the smithy and estate agent's premises seen sandwiched between terraced houses. These houses, almost facing the Baptist Church, were sited just north of Chichester Road, the entrance to which is at the southern end of the terrace.

151.   The Brunswick Dye Works in Gladys Avenue, North End, are pictured in Queen Victoria's Jubilee year, 1897. Already an established company, they were later to open works in Cressy Place, Landport, to where they transferred the dyeing and cleaning business. The North End premises then became the centre of their laundry interests.

152.   In the days of the so-called 'sweat shops', these young ladies employed at the Brunswick Works appear to be experiencing a particularly clean and comfortable working environment. The year is again 1897.

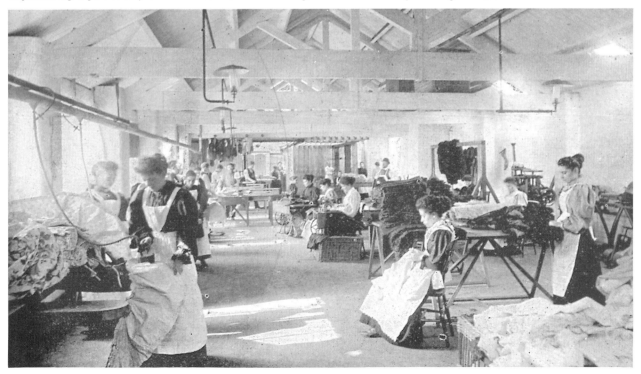

153. The German bombing of Portsmouth finally ceased on 15 July 1944 with this random strike in Newcomen Road, Stamshaw. This time, however, the destruction, which resulted in the deaths of 15 people, was caused by a V1 pilot-less flying bomb, one of only two which fell on the city (the first having destroyed properties in Locksway Road on 26 April of that year). (Reproduced with the permission of *The Portsmouth News*.)

154. An ancient location with the almost forgotten name of Shawe Cross provides the site for this obelisk. Erected in 1799, it replaced the green posts which had previously defined the boundary of the Borough of Portsmouth. A public house *The Green Posts*, now continues the tradition on a site opposite the obelisk in London Road, Hilsea.

155.  A familiar local landmark was the police box at Portsbridge. Providing essential 'aids to comfort' for the duty officer, an emergency telephone was also accessible to the general public. The Lido swimming pool is visible in the background. Brian Kingswell, P.C. 121, is the duty officer.

156. The old hamlet of Wymering is today a cul-de-sac district within Cosham and, possessing no through road, remains relatively unknown even to people who are native to Portsmouth. Located within this district of urban housing is Wymering's ancient Manor House, occupying a site which can claim both Roman and Saxon origins.

157. During the years 1900 to 1938, the Manor House was owned by Mr. Thomas Knowlys Parr, an altruistic 'squire' who was committed to charitable causes within both Wymering and Cosham. A man revered by those that knew him, his memory is perpetuated today in the recent naming of the nearby Thomas Parr House, an establishment dedicated to those people with learning difficulties.

158.   Photographs still exist recording many of the events which took place in the Manor grounds at the invitation of Mr. Parr and, on this occasion in 1933, the Portsmouth Branch of the English Folk Dance Society are demonstrating their skills.

159. Although a listed building, the Manor House was condemned to be demolished in 1959. The intervention of dedicated local councillors finally saved the fine old building from destruction. Our picture features the impressive entrance hall with its twin Jacobean staircases which date from c.1620.

160.   The funeral procession of Portsmouth's second Roman Catholic Bishop, John Baptiste Cahill, is seen making its way past Victoria Park en route to the ferry which was to transport his body for burial at Ryde in the Isle of Wight. The event was recorded on 9 August 1910.

161.   Miss Daisy Couzens, deputising for her mother the Mayoress, is seen performing her civic duty, laying the foundation stone at the Girls' Secondary School in Fawcett Road. With local dignitaries assembled beneath the scaffolding, it is perhaps worth noting that any present-day building inspector would immediately condemn the rope lashing method of securing the poles!

162. Southsea's very own Father Neptune (alias Alfred George Wilkins) was, in private life, owner of a local coach building company with premises in St Edward's Road. Seen here in just one of his several costumes, this well known local character lived in a shell-adorned house at Albert Grove, Southsea.

163. An unjustifiably neglected Portsmuthian by adoption is Father Frederick Freeley, 1881-1942. A Catholic priest, he played football for Stella F.C. (Fribourg) in the Swiss League, and on 22 November 1908 set a record by scoring 18 goals in a 24-0 victory. Following the First World War he settled in Portsmouth and did untold good work, establishing homes for orphans and deprived children in need. He also helped to found St Colman's Church in Cosham.

164.   A section of the crowd of 17,415 at Fratton Park on 1 January 1911 watching Pompey, then in the Southern League Division One, take on the might of Aston Villa of the First Division (of the Football League) in a first round F.A. Cup Tie. There was no giant killing; Villa won 4-1.

165.   A unique photograph indeed, taken in 1909, records a gathering of army veterans who had served in The Crimea, Indian Mutiny, China Uprising and Zulu War. The youngest man in the group (in uniform on the left) is a veteran of the recent Boer War! The steps of Portsmouth's Town Hall provided the setting.

166. The popularity of Southsea's 1914 Royal Counties Agricultural Show can be assessed by the vast crowd of 78,600 which attended. Declared open by the Duke and Duchess of Teck in the company of the Mayor, Alderman J.H. Corke, the show was an unqualified success, all previous attendance records being beaten.

167. In 1939, in the face of an uncertain future, the onerous task of sandbag filling at Eastney police station is shared between station staff and willing local helpers. However demanding the work, the photographer has caught them in happy mood.

168.   A wartime inspection of A.R.P. Services and Police Forces in Portsmouth was performed by the Duke of Kent on 2 April 1941. He is seen here accompanied by Admiral Sir William James C-in-C Portsmouth, Lord Mayor Sir Dennis Daley and Chief Constable A.C. West. The Duke sadly lost his life in 1942 whilst en route to Iceland, when the Sunderland flying boat in which he was travelling crashed in northern Scotland.

169. Portsmouth schools fared badly during the war years, eight being destroyed beyond repair, nine were seriously damaged and a further 11 suffered slight damage. Photographed in Arundel Street, Fratton School pictured here was one of the worst hit. The 'surface' air-raid shelter which escaped the bombing was one of many constructed in the streets of the town.

170. Portsmouth's D-Day Memorial, sited near the beach from where thousands of allied troops departed these shores for the invasion of Europe, takes the form of a simple concrete block identical to those which lined the south coast against a feared enemy landing. An unusually rare photograph, taken after the unveiling by Viscount Montgomery of Alamein, reveals an error which was not immediately recognised, i.e. the year 1945 should of course read 1944. (The *faux pas* has since been rectified!)

171. Evidence of Portsmouth's wartime air-raids can still be discovered in several locations within the city. This painted clue to the local siting of a 'Static Water Supply' was one of many indicating the presence of emergency supplies which could be used in the event of a fire blitz. This example is in Laburnum Grove, North End.

172.  This fine aerial view from the late 1950s reminds us of the many changes that have taken place in the southern part of Farlington since then. The Twilfit corset factory in the foreground has long ceased production and the Dunham Bush factory across the main road has been replaced more recently by a branch of Sainsbury's. There is no sign of the by-pass, nor of the western part of Fitzherbert Road. (Photo copyright Portsmouth City Council.)

173. So typical of Portsmouth are the grids of terraced housing found all across the city. The road running from left to right in the foreground is Winter Road, Southsea. Reginald Road Schools can be seen near the centre of the picture. Although the view was recorded in the late '50s few changes have taken place since, but we may now note the disappearance of the bus depot (near top right). (Photograph copyright Portsmouth City Council.)

174.   Another fine aerial photograph affords us a bird's eye view of Milton, *c*.1957. Note the cluster of pre-fabs at the end of Velder Avenue and the expanse of water on the left of the picture, much of which has since been reclaimed. The playing fields, with rugger and soccer goals in the centre of the view, housed a speedway track in the years prior to the Second World War. (Photograph copyright Portsmouth City Council.)